400+ FUN & UNBELIEVABLE SKATEBOARDING FACTS FOR KIDS

Contents

Introduction   4

Chapter 1: Awesome Skateboard Trick Names   6

Chapter 2: Coolest Skatepark Feature Purposes   9

Chapter 3: Superheroes: Amazing Skater Stunts   13

Chapter 4: Wildest Skateboarding Records   17

Chapter 5: Funny Skater Slang Words   20

Chapter 6: Skateboard Science: No Slipping   24

Chapter 7: Best Skateparks Around World   28

Chapter 8: Epic Skateboarding Movie Scenes   32

Chapter 9: Awesome Skateboard Art Designs   36

Chapter 10: Coolest Skateboarding Safety Gear   39

Chapter 11: Ripping Skater Girls   42

Chapter 12: Shredding Skateboarding Pets   45

Chapter 13: Virtual Skateboard Video Games   48

Chapter 14: Funniest Skateboarding Wipeouts   52

Chapter 15: Cool Skate Brand Logos   56

Chapter 16: Skateboarding Families Who Shred   60

Chapter 17: Weird Skateboard Inventions   63

Chapter 18: Skaters Giving Back Communities	66
Chapter 19: Beginner Skateboarding Trick Skills	70
Chapter 20: Skateboarding Lingo Quiz Test	74
Chapter 21: Age Records: Youngest/Oldest Skaters	78
Chapter 22: Skate Camps/Competitions for Kids	82
Chapter 23: Future of Skating: New/Cool	86
Chapter 24: Outrageous Skateboarding Mishaps	90
Chapter 25: Skaters Who Defied the Odds	94
Conclusion	98

Introduction

Get ready to embark on an epic journey through the mind-blowing world of skateboarding! This book is jam-packed with over 400 insane facts, incredible stories, and mind-bending glimpses into the future that will leave you stoked beyond belief.

First, we'll delve into the rich history and culture of skating, from the legendary skaters who paved the way to the incredible tricks that will have you saying, ""No way!"" You'll discover the wildest skateboarding records ever set, defying the laws of physics and pushing the boundaries of what's humanly possible on a board.

But that's just the start of this thrilling ride! Get ready to explore the coolest skatepark features from around the globe, each one more mind-blowing than the last. You'll feel like you're dropping into breathtaking concrete waves and soaring through the most epic skate spots on the planet.

Prepare to be blown away by the awesome power of skateboard science, as we unravel the mysteries behind how these simple planks of wood can defy gravity, build insane speeds, and let you perform mind-twisting tricks that will leave your friends in awe.

Get inspired by the incredible stories of skateboarding families who shred together, passing down their passion from generation to generation. You'll meet daring skater girls who are ripping up the scene and making their mark in a sport once dominated by boys.

Imagine the most futuristic, cutting-edge skate gear and parks that seem plucked straight from the coolest sci-fi movies. From boards that can transform into hoverboards to helmets with built-in AI coaches, this book will blow your mind with visions of skating's amazing future.

And that's just scratching the surface! Within these pages, you'll discover hilarious skater slang that will have you laughing out loud, epic movie scenes that capture the true spirit of skating, and insane skateboard inventions that will make you question reality itself.

So, strap on your helmet, grab your board, and get ready for the ride of your life! This book is your ultimate guide to the mind-blowing, adrenaline-pumping, and endlessly creative world of skateboarding. Let's shred!

Chapter 1: Awesome Skateboard Trick Names

1. The Ollie: This trick got its name from Alan "Ollie" Gelfand, who invented it in the 1970s. By snapping the tail against the ground, skaters can make their boards leap into the air, defying gravity with a simple motion.

2. The Kickflip: Imagine kicking your skateboard and making it spin beneath your feet! That's exactly what the kickflip does, thanks to a clever flick of the toes. It's like a magic trick on wheels!

3. The Varial Heelflip: This move sounds like a secret spell from a wizard's book! To perform it, skaters spin their boards horizontally while catching them with their heels. It's a true feat of coordination.

4. The Indy Grab: Grabbing the board with your hand while in mid-air might seem easy, but the Indy Grab requires precise timing and balance. It's named after the famous Independent Truck Company.

5. The Stalefish: This trick has a funny name, but there's nothing fishy about it! Skaters slide their boards across a surface, balancing on just two wheels. It's like walking a tightrope on your skateboard!

6. The Casper Flip: Ghosts might be able to walk through walls, but skaters can make their boards flip through the air with the Casper Flip! It's a spooky-sounding name for a spooky-looking trick.

7. The Boneless: Skaters don't need bones to pull off this move! They slide onto their boards from a standing position, making it look like they've become boneless contortionists.

8. The Disaster: Despite its name, this trick is far from a disaster! It's a stylish way to jump onto a skateboard, with one foot leading the way like a captain steering a ship.

9. The Primo Slide: Sliding on just two wheels might sound impossible, but skaters can do it with the Primo Slide. It's like they're balancing on a tightrope made of their skateboard trucks!

10. The Railstand: Ever seen someone stand perfectly still on their skateboard? That's the Railstand, and it takes incredible balance to pull off this stationary stunt.

11. The Caballerial: This trick has a fancy name, but it's a simple and stylish way to spin your skateboard in the air. It's like a graceful pirouette on wheels!

12. The Shuvit: Don't be fooled by the name – there's nothing shuvity about this trick! Skaters use their shoulders to spin their boards horizontally beneath their feet.

13. The Nollie: Skating backwards might seem tricky, but the Nollie makes it look easy. Skaters pop their boards into the air using their noses, launching them into some sweet reverse tricks.

14. The Fakie: This move has nothing to do with being fake! It simply means skating backwards, which can open up a whole new world of possibilities for creative tricks.

15. The Nose Manual: Balancing on just the nose of your skateboard might seem impossible, but that's exactly what skaters do with the Nose Manual. It's like walking a tightrope on wheels!

16. The Bluntslide: This trick sounds like it could cause a major injury, but it's actually a smooth way to slide along a ledge or rail using the blunt end of your skateboard.

17. The Hardflip: Don't let the name scare you – the Hardflip is just a tricky way to spin your skateboard in the air. It's like a magic trick that takes serious skill to pull off.

18. The Gazelle Flip: With a name like that, you'd expect this trick to be as graceful as a gazelle leaping across the savannah! And indeed, it's a beautiful way to flip your board beneath your feet.

19. The Darkslide: This spooky-sounding move has nothing to do with the dark! It's simply a way to slide along a ledge or rail using the nose and tail of your skateboard.

20. The Melon Grab: Forget about grabbing melons at the grocery store – this trick is all about grabbing your skateboard in mid-air! It's a fun way to add style to your airborne antics.

Chapter 2: Coolest Skatepark Feature Purposes

1. Ramps launch skaters into the air, allowing them to perform mind-blowing aerial tricks that seem to defy gravity itself. The taller and steeper the ramp, the higher and more jaw-dropping the airtime and maneuvers that can be achicved.

2. Railings offer a perfect surface for grinding, a technique where skaters slide along on the metal trucks of their boards. Mastering grinds takes precision, balance, and a whole lot of sturdy protective gear to prevent painful wipeouts.

3. Bowls mimic the shape of giant skateable pools, with smooth, concave surfaces that allow skaters to carve tight turns and build up incredible speed. As they cycle around the curved walls, skaters can feel the adrenaline rush with every lap.

4. Half-pipes, with their U-shaped ramps, launch skaters back and forth, enabling them to gain massive air with each transition. Skaters can link together complex trick combinations, spinning and flipping with every vertical ascent.

5. Stairs create the ideal obstacle for ollies and flip tricks, requiring skaters to skillfully hop from one step to the next. The more stairs, the greater the challenge – and the more impressive the feat.

6. Banks are sloped surfaces that let skaters practice their carving and turning abilities, feeling the smooth transition under their wheels as they flow from one angle to the next with precision and style.

7. Ledges offer the perfect platform for sliding and grinding tricks that test a skater's balance and accuracy to the limit. Locking into a grind on a ledge and maintaining it takes immense skill and concentration.

8. Funboxes, with their angled surfaces and multiple edges, open up endless possibilities for creative grinds, wallrides, and slick combinations. Skaters can flow from one element to the next, expressing their individuality through technical lines.

9. Quarter-pipes, with their vertical quarter-circle shape, give skaters the launch power to soar high into the air and attempt daring aerial maneuvers that will leave spectators in awe of their weightless moments of hang-time.

10. Spines combine two quarterpipes, allowing skilled skaters to transfer between them while maintaining continuous flow and momentum, linking together intricate trick sequences in a mesmerizing display of athleticism and control.

11. Hips smoothly link different obstacles together, enabling skaters to maintain their speed and momentum as they transition from one feature to the next in a seamless, fluid motion that showcases their mastery of the park's layout.

12. Pools, resembling empty swimming pools, offer a unique skating experience with vertical walls that let daring riders achieve massive air and showcase their vert skating prowess with gravity-defying maneuvers.

13. Snake runs wind back and forth in an undulating path, allowing skaters to generate serious speed and practice their lines, linking together intricate turns and adjustments as they navigate the winding course with precision.

14. Pyramids feature multiple edges and surfaces, providing the perfect platform for skaters to dial in their grinds and stall tricks, balancing with incredible poise and style as they lock into the angular obstacles.

15. Volcanoes, with their cone-shaped ramps, propel skaters skyward with a burst of launch force, enabling them to achieve massive airtime and attempt complex aerial maneuvers that will leave onlookers breathless.

16. Wallrides defy gravity, allowing skaters to ride up vertical walls and back down again in a thrilling display of skill and fearlessness that pushes the boundaries of what's possible on a board.

17. Channels are narrow paths that challenge a skater's balance and turning precision to the utmost, requiring them to make split-second adjustments and maintain control as they navigate the confined space.

18. Doorways force skaters to crouch low, requiring a smooth, controlled slide through the narrow entrance – a true test of their ability to maintain their speed and flow while adapting to the obstacle's unique challenge.

19. Embankments are sloped transitions where skaters can carve smooth turns and accelerate, feeling the momentum build as they pump their way through the banked curves with finesse and power.

20. Hubba ledges mimic street obstacles, allowing skaters to dial in their grinds and slides with pinpoint accuracy, replicating the real-world terrain they'll encounter when taking their skills to the urban landscape.

Chapter 3: Superheroes: Amazing Skater Stunts

1. With the grace of a superhero, Tony Hawk soared through the air, spinning an unbelievable 900 degrees – not just once, but two and a half full rotations! As he stuck the landing, crowds erupted in cheers for this legendary feat of aerial mastery.

2. Danny Way launched himself from a mega ramp taller than a five-story building, achieving a death-defying height that made him appear to fly like Superman. For those brief moments of hang-time, he seemed to defy the laws of gravity itself.

3. Stretching the limits of possibility, Elissa Steamer shattered records by skating an incredible 62 feet across the lips of two giant quarterpipes – a mind-boggling distance that left spectators in awe of her superhuman skills and determination.

4. Like a magician unveiling the secrets of the universe, Rodney Mullen invented tricks that appeared physically impossible, like the aptly named "impossible" and "kickflip underflip." His wizardry on a skateboard bordered on sorcery.

5. In a stunt ripped straight from the pages of a comic book, Ryan Sheckler executed a physics-defying 50-50 grind across the skids of an airborne helicopter, soaring through the sky with the powers of a true superhero.

6. Making history as the first woman to land a 9-foot flair in competition, Leticia Bufoni's incredible athletic prowess and unwavering determination solidified her status as a real-life Wonder Woman of the skateboarding world.

7. With electrifying skill and unparalleled style, Nyjah Huston dominated every skateboarding event he entered, leaving fans in awe of his superhero-like abilities that seemed to transcend the limits of mere mortals.

8. Fearlessly flying over the infamous 27-foot Alcatraz gap, Lizzie Armanto soared through the air like a caped crusader, her gravity-defying leap etching her name in the annals of skateboarding legends.

9. Blazing new trails, Mitchie Brusco achieved the unthinkable by nailing the first-ever 1080 spin on a massive quarterpipe, spinning through the air with the speed and precision of a superhuman force.

10. With a feat that seemed virtually impossible, Chris Cole executed a mind-bending flip trick, spinning his skateboard an astonishing four times in the air before somehow sticking the landing with cat-like reflexes.

11. Pushing the boundaries of women's skateboarding, Samarria Brevard made history as the first to land a 900 spin in competition, whirling through the air with the power and grace of a real-life superhero.

12. At just 12 years old, Tom Schaar achieved legendary status by landing the first-ever 1080 spin in an X Games competition, showcasing skills and bravery far beyond his years that left the world in awe.

13. Launching himself a terrifying 26 feet out of a vertical quarterpipe, Aaron "Jaws" Homoki achieved skateboarding's highest air, soaring like a superhero before miraculously returning safely to earth.

14. Wowing the world at the Tokyo Olympics, Sky Brown captured a bronze medal at the tender age of 13, her fearless skating and infectious smile inspiring fans worldwide with her superhuman talents.

15. When Rayssa Leal burst onto the scene at just 7 years old, her jaw-dropping skills and radiant charisma instantly made her a viral sensation and the superhero that every young skater aspired to become.

16. Redefining what's possible, Alex Sorgente landed a never-before-seen quadruple underflip in competition, a feat of aerial wizardry that seemed plucked straight from the realms of science fiction.

17. Paving the way for future generations, Pam Lair made history by winning the first women's vert skating event at the X Games, her trailblazing spirit and superhuman abilities inspiring legions of young skaters.

18. With technical wizardry and a graceful skating style that appeared effortless, Isamu Yamamoto mesmerized crowds, performing tricks that looked superhuman in their flawless execution.

19. In a display of sheer bravery, Brandon Westgate landed one of the biggest stair sets ever, launching down a treacherous 25-stair handrail with the courage and skill of a real-life action hero.

20. Shattering expectations, Poppy Olsen proved that girls can shred just as hard as the boys, sticking one of the highest airs ever by a female skater and cementing her status as a skateboarding superhero.

Chapter 4: Wildest Skateboarding Records

1. In a feat that defied logic, Danny Way launched himself from a mega ramp towering 65 feet high, soaring like a superhero before landing safely – a world record for the highest air on a skateboard.

2. With nerves of steel, Aaron "Jaws" Homoki achieved the longest skateboard gap jump ever, launching a jaw-dropping 26 feet across a massive quarterpipe to etch his name in the record books.

3. At just 12 years old, Tom Schaar made history by landing the first-ever 1080-degree spin in competition, whirling through the air a mind-boggling three full rotations with skills far beyond his years.

4. Pushing the boundaries of what's possible, Mitchie Brusco shattered records by nailing the first-ever 1080-degree spin on a giant quarterpipe, his aerial wizardry leaving spectators in disbelief.

5. With unwavering determination, Elissa Steamer skated an incredible 62 feet across the lips of two massive quarterpipes, setting a new world record for the longest board slide.

6. In a gravity-defying display of athleticism, Aldrin Garcia achieved the highest skateboard jump over a bar, soaring 8 feet and 2 inches above the obstacle with superhuman grace.

7. Showcasing remarkable endurance, Brandon Miaskiewicz set the world record for the longest underwater skateboard ride, gliding an astonishing 165 feet beneath the surface while holding his breath.

8. With lightning-fast footwork, Łukasz Żebrowski performed an astonishing 48 kickflips in a single minute, setting a new Guinness World Record that left onlookers in awe.

9. Defying all expectations, Samarria Brevard made history as the first woman to land a 900-degree spin in competition, whirling through the air two and a half times with trailblazing skill.

10. In a death-defying stunt, Ryan Sheckler executed a mind-bending 50-50 grind across the skids of an airborne helicopter, setting a unique world record for the craziest skateboarding trick.

11. Showcasing superhuman balance, Kai Bujak set a new world record by skateboarding on a tightrope for an incredible 72 feet, leaving spectators breathless with each precarious step.

12. With nerves of steel, Tony Hawk landed the first-ever 900-degree spin in competition at the 1999 X Games, a feat that had previously been deemed impossible and earned him legendary status.

13. Displaying remarkable precision, Kilian Martin set the world record for the most kickflips on a downrail, nailing an astonishing 25 kickflips in a single run with flawless skill.

14. In a jaw-dropping display of aerial mastery, Lizzie Armanto cleared the infamous 27-foot Alcatraz gap, setting a new world record for the highest gap jump by a female skater.

15. With superhuman stamina, Ricardo Lino set a new world record by skateboarding non-stop for an incredible 13 hours and 35 minutes, a true test of endurance and dedication.

16. Showcasing unbelievable skill, Isamu Yamamoto set a new record for the longest skateboard grind at an astounding 89 feet, balancing on his trucks with laser-like precision.

17. In a feat that pushed the limits of human ability, Aldrin Garcia set a new world record for the longest stair jump on a skateboard, launching himself an incredible 25 stairs into the history books.

18. With nerves of steel, Leticia Bufoni made history by landing the first-ever 9-foot flair, achieving a world record-setting air height that left spectators in awe of her superhuman bravery.

19. Displaying remarkable agility, Gui Khury set a new world record for the most consecutive kickflips on a rail, nailing an astonishing 17 flips in a single run without faltering.

20. In a display of sheer skill and precision, Zion Wright set a new world record by landing the first-ever quad kickflip indoors, spinning his board four full rotations in the confined space.

Chapter 5: Funny Skater Slang Words

1. "Stoked" perfectly captures that feeling of pure excitement and joy when you finally land a crazy new trick you've been working on. It's an uncontainable stoke that makes you want to pump your fist and shout in triumph!

2. Taking a "bail" means you didn't quite nail the trick and ended up falling or bailing off your skateboard in a not-so-graceful manner. Don't worry, even the pros take some gnarly bails from time to time - it's all part of progressing!

3. Oh no, you "got pitted"! This skater slang refers to landing in an awkward, contorted position after a painful wipeout. Better do some stretches before dropping in again to loosen up those twisted, rubbery bones.

4. "Sending it" means going all out without holding back, attempting an insanely difficult trick with reckless bravery and just pure skill. It's a true test of your skating abilities and sheer guts!

5. Ouch, you just "decked" out hard! Decking is the unfortunate act of taking a nasty fall directly onto the solid skateboard deck itself. That's definitely going to leave a stinging reminder - time to invest in some heavy-duty pads.

6. The ultimate compliment in skater lingo is to have "steeze" - an effortless, stylish flow and crazy trick mastery to match your laid-back, cool vibe. It's the full package that every skater aspires to.

7. That scorpion-like body bend can only mean one thing - you just epically "slammed"! A slam is a brutal, high-impact fall that probably left you dazed, seeing stars, and wishing for an undo button.

8. Watch out for that rail! If you "bonk" something, it means you crashed right into it head-on, whether it's an obstacle like a ledge or rail, or even another skater in your path.

9. Oof, looks like you really "ate it" on that one! Eating it in skater slang refers to taking an embarrassingly violent fall, probably introducing your face to the concrete in an uncomfortably intimate way.

10. "Shredding the gnar" is all about ripping it up and performing mind-blowing tricks on the gnarliest, most challenging terrain and obstacles the skatepark has to offer. It's where skills get pushed to the limit!

11. A "sketchy" trick is one that looks dangerously wobbly, unsteady or just straight-up sketch from start to finish, keeping you on the edge of your seat doubting whether the skater can actually pull it off.

12. "Coping" might sound like a therapy session, but in skatespeak it refers to those glorious metal edges on ramps and pools that skaters can grind and slide along for sparky, stylish tricks.

13. Oh no, someone's got a serious case of "chicken wings" going on! This hilarious term describes when a skater's arms are flapping wildly as they fight to regain control and balance after a near-fall.

14. To "huck" a trick is to send it into the stratosphere with reckless, fearless abandon, launching yourself skyward and hoping for the best as you wildly spin through the air.

15. Uh oh, looks like your board hung you up and left you "baconated"! A bacon happens when you somehow get stuck in an awkward, twisted position resembling a rasher of deliciously sizzling bacon. Oops!

16. "Buttering" is all about that ultra-smooth style and trick finesse. It's when skaters press down on the board to make it flex and contort like a hot, melted stick of butter. So slick!

17. If you're absolutely "mobbing" the park, it means you're a total boss - fearlessly taking on every obstacle and feature while leaving an epic trail of awesomeness and glory in your wake.

18. Every skater needs a trusty pair of "stancer pants" - those ultra-baggy, skater-approved pants with all the extra room needed for crazy leg mobility and unbeatable style when you're out shredding.

19. Looks like that board's had one too many brutal slams on the concrete! A "slam piece" is an honorary title given to skateboards that have been utterly destroyed and beaten into retirement.

20. To "rocket" a trick is to launch into a massive, sky-scraping air with explosive power, soaring majestically high like a rocket blasting off into space on a fearless voyage of aerial mastery!

Chapter 6: Skateboard Science: No Slipping

1. Skateboards might seem like simple planks of wood, but the science behind them is amazingly complex! The key is in the way the wheels are designed and positioned to create an optimal center of gravity.

2. Have you ever wondered why skateboards don't slip out from under you, even when you're riding over rough surfaces? The small, hard wheels utilize something called "rolling resistance" to grip the ground tenaciously.

3. The shape of a skateboard deck is meticulously crafted to provide the perfect balance of stiffness and flex. Too stiff, and it won't absorb impacts smoothly. Too flexible, and it loses crucial pop and responsiveness.

4. Those tiny bearings inside the skateboard wheels might look simple, but they're precision-engineered to spin with minimum friction and maximum speed. Every small detail is optimized for high-performance riding.

5. When you pop an ollie, the skateboard's unique truck geometry allows the deck to pivot and spring into the air. It's a beautiful demonstration of the principle of conservation of angular momentum in action!

6. Skateboards utilize the physics principle of rotational inertia to their advantage. The spinning wheels help stabilize the board and maintain motion, even during intense tricks and maneuvers that would normally cause instability.

7. The grip tape on a skateboard deck isn't just for looks – it's a crucial safety feature that provides traction to keep your feet firmly planted, even during the wildest aerial antics.

8. Have you noticed how skateboards seem to accelerate effortlessly when rolling down inclines? This is due to the conversion of potential energy into kinetic energy, as gravity does the hard work for you!

9. Skaters can generate incredible speeds by "pumping" their body weight in a specific motion that transfers kinetic energy to the skateboard's forward momentum. It's a masterclass in the principles of energy transfer.

10. The smooth, curved transitions of a skatepark's ramps and bowls are designed to harness the power of centripetal force, allowing skaters to defy gravity and maintain mind-blowing arcs and trajectories.

11. When a skater grinds along a rail or ledge, the metal truck axles disperse the friction and heat generated, preventing the wheels from wearing down too quickly. It's an ingenious engineering solution!

12. Skateboards are true marvels of material science. The decks are crafted from tough, flexible wood laminates, while the wheels are made from specialized polyurethane formulas to maximize grip and resilience.

13. The weight distribution and overall geometry of a skateboard are carefully calculated to make it highly maneuverable and responsive to the slightest shifts in a rider's balance and body positioning.

14. Those deep grooves in skateboard wheels, called "duromiter lines," aren't just for show – they're precisely engineered to provide optimal traction and grip on various surfaces without compromising speed.

15. When you see a skater achieving massive airtime off a vert ramp, they're harnessing the power of impulse – the force generated from the explosive ollie multiplied by the time the board is in contact with the ramp.

16. Skateboard trucks are marvels of suspension engineering, with bushings and pivot cups that allow the perfect balance of turning responsiveness and stability at high speeds and during intense tricks.

17. The curved shape of a skateboard's nose and tail aren't just for style – they're designed to reduce drag and turbulence as the board cuts through the air, maximizing speed and control.

18. Those tiny risers between the deck and trucks aren't just spacers – they're carefully calibrated to fine-tune the board's tilt and responsiveness, allowing for more technical tricks and maneuvers.

19. When you see a skater smoothly transitioning from one trick to the next, they're expertly manipulating the skateboard's center of mass to control its rotational dynamics and maintain stability.

20. Skateboards might seem like simple toys, but they're truly feats of engineering and physics. Every aspect, from the wheel size to the deck shape, is meticulously designed for optimal performance and control.

Chapter 7: Best Skateparks Around World

1. Nestled in the heart of Barcelona, the iconic Parc del Forum boasts a surreal, snake-like design that challenges skaters with its winding curves and seamless transitions. It's a skateboarder's paradise!

2. If you're craving some serious vert action, look no further than the mind-blowing Burnside Skatepark in Portland, Oregon. This legendary concrete shrine features a towering 24-foot vert wall that only the bravest souls dare conquer.

3. For a taste of skateboarding history, make a pilgrimage to the renowned Arènes de Marseille in France. This ancient Roman amphitheater has been transformed into a unique skatepark where modern tricks meet ancient architecture.

4. Denver's iconic Denver Skatepark is a sprawling concrete playground designed by skaters, for skaters. With its perfectly sculpted bowls, ledges, and creative street features, it's a mecca for skaters of all skill levels.

5. In the heart of Moscow, Russia, the Constructed Memories Skatepark stands as an impressive monument to skateboarding creativity. Its innovative design seamlessly blends art and functionality into a surreal skater's oasis.

6. For those seeking a truly unique skating experience, look no further than the FlyingBowl in Guangzhou, China. This mind-bending skatepark features a giant, suspended wooden bowl that seems to defy the laws of physics.

7. Nestled in the picturesque mountains of Whistler, Canada, the Whistler Skatepark is a breathtaking outdoor wonderland. Skaters can shred world-class terrain while surrounded by stunning natural beauty.

8. If you're after a taste of true skateboarding history, a pilgrimage to the legendary Burnside Skatepark in Portland, Oregon is a must. This iconic DIY concrete park has spawned countless legends and innovations.

9. For skaters seeking a truly surreal experience, the Piscina da Arvore in Sao Paulo, Brazil, is a must-visit. This abandoned mansion turned skatepark features a stunning pool-turned-bowl amidst a lush jungle setting.

10. In the heart of Melbourne, Australia, the Riverslide Skatepark offers a truly unique skating experience. This groundbreaking park is built into the side of a river bank, creating a one-of-a-kind urban oasis.

11. Los Angeles' legendary Venice Beach Skatepark is a true mecca for skaters worldwide. From its iconic graffiti-adorned surfaces to its perfect blend of street and transition features, it's a quintessential SoCal skating experience.

12. Nestled deep in the forests of Woodward, Pennsylvania, the legendary Camp Woodward Skatepark is a sprawling paradise for skaters of all ages and abilities. With its world-class facilities and endless terrain, it's a true skater's utopia.

13. In the heart of Copenhagen, Denmark, the Faelledparken Skatepark is a sprawling concrete wonderland designed by skaters themselves. Its creative layout and immaculate features make it a must-visit for any serious shredder.

14. For a truly surreal skating experience, venture to the stunning Black Pearl Skatepark in Haikou, China. This architectural marvel features a massive, undulating concrete structure that looks like a giant ocean wave frozen in time.

15. Berlin's infamous YAAM Skatepark is a true gem for daring skaters seeking a gritty, underground vibe. This former squatted community center features a raw, DIY aesthetic and a legendary concrete paradise.

16. Nestled in the heart of São Paulo, Brazil, the world-famous Parque da Juventude is a sprawling skatepark that attracts skaters from around the globe. Its perfectly sculpted bowls and endless street terrain make it a true mecca for the sport.

17. If you're seeking a truly unique skating experience, look no further than the mind-bending Wave Park in Xiamen, China. This surreal

concrete structure is designed to mimic the shape and flow of a massive ocean wave, challenging skaters with its undulating surfaces.

18. In the heart of Tokyo, Japan, the legendary Murasaki Park offers a true taste of urban skateboarding culture. This iconic park has spawned countless legends and is renowned for its gritty, DIY aesthetic and challenging street terrain.

19. For skaters seeking a true paradise, the Lake Cunningham Skatepark in San Jose, California, is a must-visit. This sprawling concrete oasis features endless bowls, snake runs, and perfectly sculpted transition terrain.

20. If you're craving a truly unique skating experience, make a pilgrimage to the Patinodromo de Lavapiés in Madrid, Spain. This underground skatepark is tucked away beneath the city streets, offering a surreal and gritty skating paradise.

Chapter 8: Epic Skateboarding Movie Scenes

1. In the cult classic "Dogtown and Z-Boys," the scene where the Z-Boys skate the massive waves and banks of the Pacific Ocean is a jaw-dropping display of surf-inspired skating that redefined the sport.

2. Who could forget the intense "stairs" sequence in "Police Story 3" where Jackie Chan performs a mind-blowing stunt, skating down an incredibly long set of stairs while fighting off bad guys with his signature martial arts skills?

3. In "Lords of Dogtown," the recreation of the legendary Zephyr Team's backyard pool sessions perfectly captures the raw, rebellious spirit of skateboarding's early days and the birth of vert skating.

4. The "Muir Skate Ranch" scene in "Thrashin'" is a true celebration of '80s skateboarding culture, featuring an epic game of skate and some of the most outrageous tricks and fashion of the era.

5. Who could forget the iconic "Venice Beach" scene in "Lords of Dogtown," where the Z-Boys take their revolutionary style and attitude to the iconic beachfront skate mecca?

6. The "Underground Skate Session" in "Grind" is a thrilling showcase of urban skating, as the characters navigate a surreal, subterranean skatepark filled with mind-bending obstacles and features.

7. In "Wassup Rockers," the intense "Hill Bomb" scene perfectly captures the adrenaline-fueled world of downhill skateboarding, as the characters fearlessly bomb down steep city streets at breakneck speeds.

8. The "X Games" sequence in "XxX" is a heart-pounding spectacle, featuring extreme sports legend Travis Pastrana performing death-defying skateboard stunts and tricks on a colossal, custom-built mega ramp.

9. The "Hallway Havoc" scene in "Brink!" is a quintessential '90s skateboarding moment, as the characters shred through a high school's hallways, performing creative tricks on every obstacle in their path.

10. In "Skate Kitchen," the raw, gritty skating scenes perfectly capture the authentic spirit of New York's vibrant skate culture and the empowering camaraderie of its female skaters.

11. The "Downhill Chase" in "Jackass: The Movie" is a hilarious and heart-pounding spectacle, as the Jackass crew attempts to outrun a rampaging bison on their skateboards, resulting in pure chaos.

12. The "Carlsbad Gap" scene in "Lords of Dogtown" is a legendary moment in skateboarding history, recreating the iconic stunt where Alan "Ollie" Gelfand launched himself over a terrifying 20-foot gap.

13. In "Kids," the gritty skating scenes in New York's Washington Square Park offer a raw and authentic glimpse into the city's vibrant skateboarding subculture of the '90s.

14. The "Skateboard Bullfighting" scene in "Hot Rod" is a hilarious and absurd take on extreme sports, as the characters attempt to out-maneuver an angry bull on their skateboards.

15. The "Skate Escape" sequence in "Paranoid Park" perfectly captures the thrill and freedom of skateboarding through the eyes of a troubled teen, as he navigates the city's urban terrain and obstacles.

16. In "Mid90s," the authentic recreation of '90s skateboarding culture and the bond between a group of skater kids in Los Angeles is both hilarious and heartwarming.

17. The "School Yard Skate" scene in "Grind" showcases some of the most creative and outrageous skateboarding tricks, as the characters turn an ordinary schoolyard into their personal skatepark.

18. In "The Lords of Flatbush," the iconic opening scene features the characters skating through the streets of Brooklyn, perfectly capturing the rebellious spirit of '70s skateboarding culture.

19. The "Rooftop Escape" in "Teenage Mutant Ninja Turtles II: The Secret of the Ooze" is a thrilling and imaginative sequence, as the Turtles use their skateboarding skills to evade capture and perform gravity-defying stunts across the city's rooftops.

20. In "The Secret Life of Walter Mitty," the scene where Walter daydreams about becoming a daring skateboarder performing mind-blowing tricks in stunning Iceland landscapes is a visually stunning celebration of the sport's potential for adventure and fantasy.

Chapter 9: Awesome Skateboard Art Designs

1. Imagine a skateboard deck that looks like a cosmic explosion, with vibrant swirls of color and intricate patterns that seem to dance across the surface. It's a true masterpiece on wheels!

2. Picture a skateboard adorned with fierce, larger-than-life illustrations of mythical dragons, their scales glistening with metallic hues and their fierce eyes daring you to shred like a true warrior.

3. Envision a deck that's a mesmerizing optical illusion, with mind-bending geometric patterns that seem to shift and move as you ride, creating a trippy, otherworldly experience.

4. Imagine a skateboard covered in stunning nature scenes, with lush forests, majestic mountains, and cascading waterfalls captured in exquisite detail, inviting you to shred through nature's wonders.

5. Picture a deck that's a vibrant celebration of your favorite superheroes, with bold illustrations and comic book-inspired graphics that make you feel like you're part of their epic adventures.

6. Envision a skateboard that looks like a work of intricate henna art, with delicate, swirling patterns and intricate designs that mesmerize the eye with their beauty and complexity.

7. Imagine a deck that's a breathtaking underwater scene, with colorful coral reefs, exotic fish, and mysterious deep-sea creatures brought to life in stunning detail.

8. Picture a skateboard that's a masterpiece of abstract expressionism, with bold brushstrokes, splashes of vibrant color, and a canvas that seems to come alive beneath your feet.

9. Envision a deck that celebrates your favorite video game or anime characters, with detailed illustrations and graphics that transport you into their exciting virtual worlds.

10. Imagine a skateboard that's a stunning celestial scene, with swirling galaxies, twinkling stars, and mysterious nebulae that make you feel like you're riding through the cosmos.

11. Picture a deck that's a mesmerizing kaleidoscope of patterns and shapes, with intricate designs that create a dazzling, ever-changing visual spectacle as you ride.

12. Envision a skateboard that's a tribute to your favorite band or musician, with iconic album covers, song lyrics, and bold graphics that let you rock out while you shred.

13. Imagine a deck that's a vibrant celebration of your cultural heritage, with traditional art, symbols, and designs that honor your roots and inspire pride with every ride.

14. Picture a skateboard that's a whimsical, fairy-tale scene, with enchanting illustrations of mythical creatures, magical forests, and fanciful castles that ignite your imagination.

15. Envision a deck that's a sleek and stylish blend of geometric shapes, bold colors, and minimalist design elements, creating a modern and eye-catching aesthetic.

16. Imagine a skateboard that's a jaw-dropping 3D masterpiece, with intricate carvings, textures, and layers that seem to leap off the surface and transport you to another dimension.

17. Picture a deck that's a vibrant and energetic graffiti mural, with bold strokes, vibrant colors, and street art styles that capture the raw, rebellious spirit of skateboarding culture.

18. Envision a skateboard that's a mesmerizing mandala design, with intricate patterns, symbols, and colors that create a sense of harmony and balance as you ride.

19. Imagine a deck that's a stunning tribute to your favorite artist or art movement, with iconic paintings, styles, and motifs that transform your skateboard into a rolling canvas.

20. Picture a skateboard that's a captivating display of mind-bending optical illusions, with patterns and designs that seem to shift and morph before your eyes, challenging your perception with every roll.

Chapter 10: Coolest Skateboarding Safety Gear

1. Imagine a helmet that looks like it's straight out of a futuristic sci-fi movie, with sleek, aerodynamic lines and vibrant LED lights that illuminate the park in a mesmerizing glow.

2. Picture knee pads that are adorned with bold superhero emblems, making you feel invincible as you soar through the air and conquer even the gnarliest of obstacles.

3. Envision elbow pads that look like they've been plucked from the armor of a medieval knight, with intricate designs and sturdy construction to protect you during every epic battle on the board.

4. Imagine wrist guards that resemble the sleek, mechanical exoskeletons of a futuristic cyborg, providing unparalleled support and flexibility as you push the limits of your skating abilities.

5. Picture a full-face mask that transforms you into a fearsome creature from another realm, with fierce, otherworldly designs that strike awe into the hearts of onlookers.

6. Envision a helmet that's a mesmerizing kaleidoscope of vibrant colors and intricate patterns, creating a dazzling display that captivates the eye with every revolution.

7. Imagine shin guards that look like they've been crafted from the scales of a mighty dragon, with intricate textures and a fierce, reptilian aesthetic that demands respect.

8. Picture elbow pads that celebrate your favorite video game or anime characters, with detailed illustrations and graphics that transport you into their exciting virtual worlds.

9. Envision a full suit of body armor that looks like it was forged in the heart of a volcano, with molten colors, fiery textures, and a design that radiates pure power and intensity.

10. Imagine a helmet that's a stunning work of abstract art, with bold brushstrokes, splashes of vibrant color, and a canvas that transforms your head into a masterpiece.

11. Picture wrist guards that resemble the intricate patterns and designs found in ancient civilizations, with symbols and motifs that honor your cultural heritage with every roll.

12. Envision knee pads that look like they've been crafted from the sleek, iridescent shells of mystical deep-sea creatures, with mesmerizing colors and textures that shimmer and shine.

13. Imagine a full-face mask that transforms you into a fearsome creature from the depths of the ocean, with intricate details and a design that captures the raw power and majesty of the deep.

14. Picture a helmet that's a mesmerizing optical illusion, with mind-bending patterns and designs that seem to shift and morph before your eyes, challenging your perception with every ride.

15. Envision shin guards that celebrate the beauty and majesty of nature, with vibrant illustrations of lush forests, majestic mountains, and cascading waterfalls that transport you into the great outdoors.

16. Imagine elbow pads that look like they've been crafted from the sleek, aerodynamic curves of a high-tech spacecraft, with a futuristic design that allows you to soar through the skatepark with ease.

17. Picture wrist guards that resemble the intricate patterns and textures found in traditional henna designs, with delicate swirls and motifs that add a touch of elegance and beauty to your gear.

18. Envision a full suit of body armor that's a stunning celestial scene, with swirling galaxies, twinkling stars, and mysterious nebulae that make you feel like you're skating through the cosmos.

19. Imagine a helmet that celebrates your favorite band or musician, with iconic album covers, song lyrics, and bold graphics that let you rock out while you shred in style.

20. Picture knee pads that are adorned with fierce, larger-than-life illustrations of mythical creatures, with their scales glistening with metallic hues and their fierce eyes daring you to push your limits.

Chapter 11: Ripping Skater Girls

1. With unshakable determination etched across her face, Rayssa Leal defied expectations, becoming a viral sensation at just 7 years old with her gravity-defying tricks and infectious smile.

2. Fearlessly soaring over massive gaps, Lizzie Armanto's trailblazing spirit and unwavering grit have made her a true icon, shattering records and inspiring a new generation of skater girls.

3. With a style as smooth as silk, Lacey Baker flows through the park, her technical wizardry and graceful lines leaving crowds in awe of her artistic finesse on the board.

4. At just 13 years old, Sky Brown captured the world's attention, fearlessly shredding her way to an Olympic bronze medal and proving that age is no barrier to greatness.

5. Leticia Bufoni's fearless determination is matched only by her incredible skill, as she continues to break boundaries and land mind-blowing tricks that redefine what's possible for women in the sport.

6. With a contagious positive energy that radiates from her huge smile, Samarria Brevard inspires everyone around her as she pushes the limits of women's skateboarding with her incredible talent.

7. Elissa Steamer's unwavering focus and passion for skating have propelled her to new heights, as she continually shatters records and leaves spectators in awe of her incredible abilities.

8. Like a whirlwind of energy and style, Mariah Duran attacks the park with a fierceness that demands respect, her technical prowess and creativity cementing her status as a true force in women's skating.

9. With a grace and elegance that belies her power, Nora Vasconcellos flows effortlessly through the most challenging terrain, her smooth style and immense skill captivating audiences worldwide.

10. Pamela Rosa's relentless work ethic and unwavering passion have propelled her to the forefront of women's skating, her incredible talent and determination inspiring countless others to follow their dreams.

11. Showcasing incredible athleticism and skill, Brighton Zeuner's fearless approach to skating has earned her a place among the greats, as she continues to push the boundaries of what's possible.

12. With a style that seamlessly blends raw power and artistic expression, Alana Smith's skating is a true spectacle to behold, her innovative tricks and unique flair leaving a lasting impression.

13. Jordyn Barratt's infectious energy and love for skating radiate from every move she makes, inspiring others with her positive attitude and incredible talent on the board.

14. Like a force of nature, Alexis Sablone commands the park with her technical precision and unwavering determination, her incredible skills and accomplishments solidifying her status as a true trailblazer.

15. With a grace and poise that defies gravity, Sakura Yosozumi's smooth style and effortless execution have made her a rising star in the world of women's skating.

16. Hayley Wilson's fearless spirit and relentless drive have propelled her to new heights, as she continues to push the boundaries and inspire others with her incredible talent.

17. With a fierce determination and unwavering focus, Aori Nishimura's technical mastery and creative flair have earned her a place among the elite, inspiring a new generation of skaters to follow their dreams.

18. Yndiara Asp's infectious energy and passion for skating are evident in every move she makes, as she defies expectations and leaves crowds in awe of her incredible skills.

19. Like a graceful ballet dancer on wheels, Momiji Nishiya's fluid style and artistic expression have captivated audiences worldwide, cementing her status as a true phenomenon in women's skating.

20. With a fiery determination and unshakable confidence, Lore Bruggeman attacks the park with a fearlessness that demands respect, her incredible talent and unique style inspiring skaters of all ages.

Chapter 12: Shredding Skateboarding Pets

1. With a wagging tail and boundless energy, Bambam the bulldog defies expectations, shredding the park with his unique four-legged style and infectious enthusiasm for skating.

2. Gracefully gliding across the concrete, Didga the cat showcases her feline agility and balance, nailing tricks that leave humans in awe of her skateboarding prowess.

3. Undeterred by his small stature, Motty the chihuahua fearlessly tackles every obstacle, his tenacious spirit and determination inspiring skaters of all sizes to follow their dreams.

4. With a mane of flowing fur and a love for speed, Chilli the horse gallops onto the scene, seamlessly transitioning from the racetrack to the skatepark with ease.

5. Roo the kangaroo bounds through the park, her powerful legs propelling her skyward as she executes gravity-defying tricks that defy the laws of physics.

6. Harnessing the grace and poise of his species, Squeak the squirrel effortlessly shreds the park, his nimble movements and fearless spirit captivating audiences worldwide.

7. With a fluffy coat and a contagious smile, Rama the sheepdog glides across the concrete, her gentle demeanor and natural talent making her a beloved icon in the skate community.

8. Undaunted by his large size, Bruno the bear lumbers through the park, his raw power and agility on display as he tackles obstacles with ease.

9. Gliding across the pavement with the elegance of a prima ballerina, Tutu the swan showcases her unique skateboarding style, leaving spectators in awe of her grace and poise.

10. With a mischievous twinkle in his eye, Ripper the raccoon fearlessly navigates the park, his dexterity and problem-solving skills making him a formidable force on four wheels.

11. Harnessing the speed and agility of her species, Flash the cheetah blurs across the concrete, her lightning-fast reflexes and incredible precision leaving onlookers breathless.

12. Undeterred by his small stature, Zippy the mouse fearlessly tackles the park, his determination and unwavering spirit inspiring skaters of all ages to chase their dreams.

13. With a majestic presence and a regal demeanor, Raja the elephant gracefully glides through the park, her gentle nature and immense strength making her a true ambassador for the sport.

14. Harnessing the power and grace of the equine species, Blaze the zebra seamlessly navigates the park, her unique stripes and incredible athleticism captivating audiences worldwide.

15. With a playful attitude and boundless energy, Ollie the otter shreds the park with ease, his aquatic agility and natural talent making him a true sensation in the skate community.

16. Undaunted by his hulking size, Tank the rhinoceros charges through the park, his thick skin and unwavering determination serving as an inspiration to never give up.

17. With a majestic presence and a regal bearing, Simba the lion prowls through the park, his powerful movements and fearless spirit commanding respect from all who witness his skating prowess.

18. Harnessing the grace and agility of her species, Lexi the fox effortlessly weaves through the park, her quick reflexes and cunning nature making her a formidable force on four wheels.

19. With a gentle demeanor and a love for adventure, Buddy the goat fearlessly tackles every obstacle, his playful spirit and unwavering determination inspiring skaters of all ages.

20. Undaunted by his unusual appearance, Spike the porcupine rolls through the park with confidence, his sharp quills and unique style making him a true standout in the skate community.

Chapter 13: Virtual Skateboard Video Games

1. Imagine stepping into a virtual world where the laws of physics are mere suggestions, allowing you to defy gravity and perform the most mind-bending tricks imaginable on your digital skateboard.

2. Picture a game that transports you to a futuristic cityscape, where you can grind along hovering neon rails and launch yourself off towering skyscrapers into the digital stratosphere.

3. Envision a virtual skatepark that morphs and transforms before your eyes, constantly challenging you with new obstacles and terrain that push the boundaries of what's possible on four wheels.

4. Imagine a game that allows you to create and customize your own unique skater avatar, from their outrageous hairstyles to their signature trick combos that leave the virtual crowds in awe.

5. Picture a world where you can team up with your friends online, shredding through fantastical realms and competing in epic skate battles to determine who truly rules the digital halfpipe.

6. Envision a game that transports you to iconic real-world skate spots, from the legendary streets of Barcelona to the massive vert ramps of the X Games, all rendered in stunning detail.

7. Imagine a virtual reality experience that puts you directly on the board, allowing you to feel the rush of wind and the thrill of catching massive air with every trick you land.

8. Picture a game that blends the art of skateboarding with the thrill of high-speed racing, challenging you to navigate twisting tracks and pull off sick combos while outpacing your opponents.

9. Envision a world where you can skate through the pages of your favorite comic book or movie universe, grinding along gargoyles and shredding through fantastical environments straight out of your wildest dreams.

10. Imagine a game that allows you to build and design your own skatepark from the ground up, crafting the perfect digital playground to hone your skills and unleash your creativity.

11. Picture a virtual world where the only limit is your imagination, as you skate through surreal dreamscapes and otherworldly realms that defy the boundaries of reality itself.

12. Envision a game that combines the thrill of skateboarding with the strategy of puzzle-solving, challenging you to navigate mind-bending obstacle courses and unravel hidden secrets with every ollied fence and grind.

13. Imagine a world where you can embark on an epic skateboarding adventure, exploring vast open worlds and completing daring missions while perfecting your skills and progressing your character's abilities.

14. Picture a game that allows you to create and share your own custom skateboarding levels with players around the globe, fostering a vibrant online community of creative skaters.

15. Envision a virtual reality experience that immerses you in the heart of a bustling skate scene, where you can interact with other players, trade tricks, and compete in impromptu skate-offs.

16. Imagine a game that blends the artistry of skateboarding with the intensity of combat, allowing you to battle opponents with your board while unleashing a barrage of tricks and combos.

17. Picture a world where your skateboard transforms into a futuristic hoverboard, enabling you to soar through the skies and explore vast aerial environments filled with ramps and grind rails in the clouds.

18. Envision a game that combines the thrill of skateboarding with the intensity of survival, challenging you to navigate treacherous post-apocalyptic landscapes while outrunning hostile threats and scavenging for resources.

19. Imagine a virtual reality experience that transports you to the most iconic skate spots from around the globe, allowing you to shred legendary terrain without ever leaving your living room.

20. Picture a game that blends the artistry of skateboarding with the creativity of music creation, enabling you to compose sick beats and rhythms by landing tricks and combos in perfect sync.

Chapter 14: Funniest Skateboarding Wipeouts

1. Imagine the hilarity of a skater attempting a massive stair set, only to slip on a banana peel mid-trick, sending them tumbling down in a comical blur of flailing limbs and airborne accessories.

2. Picture the scene of a skater confidently dropping into a bowl, only to realize too late that their shoelaces are untied, resulting in a tangled mess of human and board as they face-plant spectacularly.

3. Envision the comedy of a skater attempting to impress a group of onlookers with a daring trick, only to have their pants suddenly split, leaving them to complete the maneuver while desperately trying to maintain their modesty.

4. Imagine the hilarity of a skater misjudging the height of a launch ramp, soaring majestically through the air before landing in an unexpected and undignified belly flop on the flat ground beyond.

5. Picture the scene of a skater confidently grinding a rail, only to have a mischievous squirrel dart across their path, causing them to lose balance and comically pinwheel off the side in a tangle of limbs.

6. Envision the comedy of a skater attempting an ambitious trick over a gap, only to have their board inexplicably detach mid-air, sending them crashing down in a bewildered heap while their rogue deck continues its own separate flight path.

7. Imagine the hilarity of a skater attempting to navigate a tight snake run, only to misjudge a turn and find themselves comically wedged between the walls, legs flailing helplessly in the air.

8. Picture the scene of a skater confidently dropping into a pool, only to have their board shoot out from underneath them, leaving them to slide down the vertical walls in a hapless, belly-flopping descent.

9. Envision the comedy of a skater attempting to grind a ledge, only to have their baggy pants catch on the edge, resulting in a comical and undignified de-pantsing as they tumble off in surprise.

10. Imagine the hilarity of a skater attempting a complex flip trick, only to have a rogue gust of wind send their board spiraling off in an unexpected direction, leaving them to land awkwardly and scramble after their runaway deck.

11. Picture the scene of a skater confidently launching off a vert ramp, only to have a sudden wardrobe malfunction leave them desperately clutching at their clothing mid-air while trying to maintain their composure.

12. Envision the comedy of a skater attempting to show off their skills at a crowded park, only to have their board inexplicably start rolling away, sending them comically chasing after it while onlookers roar with laughter.

13. Imagine the hilarity of a skater attempting a daring gap jump, only to land directly in a conveniently placed puddle, sending a comical splash erupting into the air as they emerge dripping and bewildered.

14. Picture the scene of a skater confidently dropping into a bowl, only to have their headphones become tangled around their legs, resulting in a comical tangle of limbs and cords as they struggle to maintain their balance.

15. Envision the comedy of a skater attempting to impress a group of spectators with a complex trick, only to have their board inexplicably launch directly into their own face, leaving them dazed and spinning on the ground.

16. Imagine the hilarity of a skater attempting to grind a ledge, only to have their loose-fitting shorts suddenly fall down mid-trick, forcing them to complete the maneuver while frantically clutching at their waistband.

17. Picture the scene of a skater confidently launching off a vert ramp, only to have a rogue gust of wind catch their shirt, causing it to comically billow up and obscure their vision mid-air, resulting in a bewildered crash landing.

18. Envision the comedy of a skater attempting to navigate a tight transition, only to comically lose their balance and start spinning uncontrollably, arms flailing wildly as they struggle to regain control.

19. Imagine the hilarity of a skater attempting to impress a group of onlookers with a daring trick, only to have their board inexplicably shoot out from underneath them, sending them tumbling backwards in a comical display of flailing limbs.

20. Picture the scene of a skater confidently dropping into a pool, only to have their shorts suddenly split down the back mid-trick, leaving them to complete the maneuver with a comically exposed backside while desperately trying to maintain their dignity.

Chapter 15: Cool Skate Brand Logos

1. Imagine a bold logo featuring a fierce dragon, its scales shimmering with metallic hues and intricate details that capture the raw power and energy of this mythical creature.

2. Picture a sleek logo with clean lines and a minimalist aesthetic, showcasing a stylized graphic that evokes a sense of speed and fluidity, reflecting the grace and flow of skateboarding itself.

3. Envision a vibrant logo that celebrates nature's beauty, featuring intricate illustrations of lush foliage, winding vines, and vibrant flowers that seamlessly blend the natural world with the artistry of skateboarding.

4. Imagine a rugged logo that pays homage to the gritty, urban roots of skateboarding, with bold typography and grungy textures that capture the raw energy of city streets and DIY skate spots.

5. Picture a whimsical logo that transports you to a realm of fantasy, featuring imaginative illustrations of mythical creatures, magical landscapes, and surreal elements that spark the imagination.

6. Envision a logo that fuses ancient and modern elements, with intricate patterns and symbols inspired by various cultures, blending the rich tapestry of global traditions with the contemporary spirit of skateboarding.

7. Imagine a bold logo that channels the spirit of rock'n'roll, with edgy graphics and a rebellious attitude that perfectly encapsulates the countercultural roots of skateboarding culture.

8. Picture a sleek, futuristic logo that looks like it belongs in a science fiction movie, with streamlined shapes and innovative design elements that evoke a sense of cutting-edge technology and progress.

9. Envision a logo that celebrates the rich artistic heritage of skateboarding, featuring intricate calligraphic lettering and ornate embellishments inspired by various artistic movements and styles.

10. Imagine a playful logo that captures the joy and freedom of skateboarding, with vibrant colors, whimsical illustrations, and a sense of childlike wonder and imagination.

11. Picture a rugged logo that evokes the great outdoors, with earthy tones, textured graphics, and natural elements that celebrate the harmony between skateboarding and the natural world.

12. Envision a bold logo that pays homage to the golden age of skateboarding, with retro graphics, vintage typography, and nostalgic elements that transport you back to the sport's iconic roots.

13. Imagine a sleek logo with a minimalist aesthetic, featuring clean lines, geometric shapes, and a sense of balance and symmetry that reflects the technical precision of skateboarding tricks and maneuvers.

14. Picture a vibrant logo that celebrates diversity and inclusivity, with colorful graphics, uplifting imagery, and a welcoming vibe that invites people of all backgrounds to join the skateboarding community.

15. Envision a logo that combines classic and modern elements, blending vintage skateboarding aesthetics with contemporary design trends to create a timeless and stylish look.

16. Imagine a bold logo that celebrates the spirit of adventure and exploration, featuring rugged graphics, dynamic lines, and a sense of movement that captures the thrill of discovering new skate spots and pushing personal boundaries.

17. Picture a sleek logo with a futuristic vibe, featuring sleek typography, innovative design elements, and a sense of cutting-edge technology that evokes the idea of pushing the boundaries of skateboarding into new and exciting realms.

18. Envision a vibrant logo that celebrates the diversity of skateboarding cultures around the world, featuring intricate patterns, vibrant colors, and unique design elements inspired by various traditions and art styles.

19. Imagine a rugged logo that captures the raw energy and grit of street skating, with bold graphics, graffiti-inspired elements, and a sense of urban edginess that reflects the rebellious spirit of skateboarding's underground roots.

20. Picture a bold logo that celebrates the artistry and creativity of skateboarding, featuring dynamic illustrations, expressive typography, and a sense of movement and fluidity that captures the beauty and grace of the sport.

Chapter 16: Skateboarding Families Who Shred

1. With a shared passion that spans generations, the Rodriguez family takes to the park as a tight-knit crew, cheering each other on as grandpa, dad, and little Mia effortlessly shred the bowls and rails.

2. The Nguyen siblings rule the streets, with big brother Tuan leading the charge as little sisters Mai and Linh fearlessly follow his lines, their bond as unbreakable as their determination to push each other's skills.

3. In the Moore household, skateboarding is a family affair, with dad Joe and mom Kristen instilling their love for the sport in young twins Luke and Leah from the moment they could push.

4. The Yamamoto clan is a force to be reckoned with, as patriarch Akira and his sons Hideaki and Kenji flow through the park with a three-generational style that leaves crowds in awe.

5. For the close-knit Jackson family, the skatepark is their second home, where dad Terrence and mom Keisha casually cruise alongside daughters Nia and Zuri, their infectious laughter echoing off the concrete.

6. The Ramirez brothers, Carlos and Diego, have been shredding since they were knee-high, with their proud parents cheering them on as the unstoppable duo tear up every obstacle in their path.

7. In the tight-knit Garcia family, skateboarding is more than just a hobby – it's a way of life. Mom, dad, and kids Emilio and Sofia hit the park like a well-oiled machine.

8. The daring Patel sisters, Rani and Ariyana, have been skating circles around the boys since day one, with their parents Raj and Anjali beaming with pride at their fearless daughters' skills.

9. For the adventurous Kovács clan, family skate sessions are a beloved tradition, with mom Erzsébet and dad István leading sons Zoltán and Ákos on exciting trips to shred parks around the world.

10. In the lively Kelly household, the whole family gets in on the action, with mom Shannon and dad Mike cheering on kids Rylie and Brody as they effortlessly flow through the concrete playground.

11. The unstoppable O'Connor siblings, Liam and Maeve, have been skating since they could walk, with their parents Seamus and Fiona lovingly fostering their daring children's passion for the sport.

12. At the local park, the Torres family is a familiar sight, with dad Miguel and mom Lourdes encouraging their fearless kids Alejandro and Isabella to push their limits and have fun.

13. For the close-knit Larsson family, skateboarding is a shared language, with mom Ingrid and dad Lars seamlessly keeping up with their talented sons Erik and Nils as they shred the bowls.

14. The daring Patel brothers, Arjun and Rohan, have been rivals on the board since birth, with their proud parents Vikram and Sonia cheering them on as they engage in good-natured skate battles.

15. In the lively Soto household, skateboarding is a way of life, with mom Carmen and dad Julio leading their energetic kids Marco and Lucia on epic skate adventures around the city.

16. The unstoppable Dubois sisters, Amélie and Colette, rule the park with their graceful yet powerful style, their proud parents Giselle and Henri beaming as their daughters showcase their skills.

17. For the fun-loving Russo family, the skatepark is a playground where mom Francesca and dad Luca join their kids Matteo and Gia in perfecting new tricks and laughing off the inevitable falls.

18. The tight-knit Gonzalez clan is a force to be reckoned with, as dad Jorge and mom Rosario effortlessly keep up with their fearless sons Mateo and Javier on the concrete waves.

19. In the lively Hernandez household, skateboarding is a family tradition, with dad Carlos and mom Mariana passing down their love of the sport to their talented kids Gabriela and Diego.

20. The unstoppable Kim siblings, Jae and Hana, have been shredding together since they were tots, with their proud parents Young and Miyeok cheering them on as they push each other's skills to new heights.

Chapter 17: Weird Skateboard Inventions

1. Imagine a skateboard that can actually levitate and defy gravity, using advanced magnetic technology to let you soar effortlessly over any terrain or obstacle in your path!

2. Picture a board that's powered by a compact jet engine, propelling you at incredible speeds while you carve through the air like a superhero soaring through the skyline.

3. Envision a skateboard that can split into separate pieces and transform into a handy mode of transport, like a sleek rocket pack or a futuristic hoverboard at the click of a button.

4. Imagine a board with built-in artificial intelligence that can analyze your riding style and provide real-time coaching to help you perfect tricks and improve your skills.

5. Picture a skateboard with a revolutionary new wheel design that can actually grip to walls and ceilings, letting you defy gravity and shred vertically in mind-bending new ways.

6. Envision a board that harnesses the power of cutting-edge drone technology, enabling you to catch massive air while the built-in propellers stabilize your flight for perfect landings.

7. Imagine a skateboard with a compact, retractable sail that can capture wind power, giving you an extra boost of speed as you surf across land and sea!

8. Picture a board made from a futuristic smart material that can actually repair itself after crashes, ensuring your deck stays in pristine condition no matter how gnarly the bail.

9. Envision a skateboard with an augmented reality display that can project breathtaking virtual environments all around you as you ride, immersing you in fantastic digital worlds.

10. Imagine a board that uses powerful electromagnets to reduce friction, enabling you to glide across any surface with the greatest of ease and reach insane top speeds.

11. Picture a skateboard that can split into multiple pieces and reconfigure itself for different terrains, transforming from a traditional deck to an all-terrain off-road board at a moment's notice.

12. Envision a board made from a revolutionary smart material that can actually change its shape and contours to match your preferences or the demands of different tricks.

13. Imagine a skateboard with built-in holographic technology that can scan and digitally map out the perfect lines for you to follow through the most complex skate environments.

14. Picture a board that generates an invisible force field around you, providing full-body protection from falls and impacts without the need for traditional safety gear.

15. Envision a skateboard made from a cutting-edge material lighter than air, enabling you to float and carve through the sky like a majestic bird in flight.

16. Imagine a board that can harness the power of the sun, with solar panels that charge an built-in electric motor to provide an extra boost of speed on demand.

17. Picture a skateboard with a compact teleportation device that can instantly transport you and your board across short distances, letting you bend space for the perfect trick runs.

18. Envision a board that uses advanced haptic technology to simulate any terrain or surface beneath your wheels through subtle vibrations and feedback in the deck.

19. Imagine a skateboard with a brain-computer interface that can read your thoughts and intentions, executing tricks and maneuvers with just the power of your mind.

20. Picture a board made from a revolutionary self-cooling material that can actually chill itself during intense riding sessions, providing a refreshing, friction-free glide.

Chapter 18: Skaters Giving Back Communities

1. With a passion for helping others, a group of skaters came together to build a brand-new skatepark in their local community center, providing a safe and inclusive space for kids to learn, grow, and discover the joy of skating.

2. After a devastating natural disaster struck their town, a crew of skaters didn't hesitate to lend a hand, using their boards to transport supplies and aid to those in need with a smile on their faces.

3. Recognizing the power of mentorship, a team of experienced skaters volunteered their time to teach skateboarding clinics at underprivileged schools, inspiring the next generation to chase their dreams on four wheels.

4. When a nearby children's hospital was in need of funds, a group of skaters organized an epic skating exhibition, wowing the crowd with jaw-dropping tricks while raising money for a worthy cause.

5. Determined to make a difference, a passionate skater started a nonprofit organization that provides skateboarding lessons and equipment to underprivileged youth, fostering confidence and life skills through the sport they love.

6. After a local skatepark fell into disrepair, a dedicated crew of skaters rallied their community to clean up and restore the beloved spot, breathing new life into the concrete canvas they call home.

7. Recognizing the importance of environmental stewardship, a group of eco-conscious skaters organized regular park clean-ups, ensuring their local skate spots remain pristine havens for years to come.

8. When a young skater was struggling with personal challenges, a kind-hearted pro took them under their wing, offering mentorship and support to help them find their way through the power of skateboarding.

9. In the wake of a tragic event, a community of skaters came together to honor the memory of a fallen friend by creating a beautiful mural at their local park, celebrating their shared love for the sport.

10. Determined to spread joy, a group of skaters visited local retirement homes, putting on lively demonstrations and sharing stories that brought smiles to the faces of the residents.

11. After learning about food insecurity in their neighborhood, a compassionate crew of skaters organized a food drive at their local skatepark, collecting donations to support families in need.

12. Recognizing the transformative power of art, a collective of creative skaters collaborated with local artists to beautify a once-neglected skate spot, turning it into a vibrant outdoor gallery.

13. When a community center was facing budget cuts, a group of skaters stepped up to the plate, organizing a fundraising event that helped keep the doors open and programs running.

14. With a passion for inclusivity, a team of skaters launched a mentorship program that paired experienced riders with individuals facing physical or cognitive challenges, empowering them through the sport.

15. After learning about the challenges faced by homeless youth, a group of skaters organized a clothing and supply drive, collecting essentials to support those in need within their community.

16. Recognizing the importance of environmental conservation, a crew of nature-loving skaters volunteered their time to help maintain and preserve local hiking trails, ensuring future generations can enjoy the great outdoors.

17. When a local animal shelter was struggling, a compassionate group of skaters hosted a pet adoption event at their park, finding loving homes for countless furry friends in need.

18. With a passion for education, a team of skaters visited local schools, using their skills and stories to inspire students and promote the values of perseverance and determination.

19. After witnessing the struggles of veterans in their community, a grateful group of skaters organized a charity event, raising funds to support programs that assist those who have served their country.

20. Recognizing the power of sport to bring people together, a diverse crew of skaters hosted a community skate jam, fostering unity and celebrating the shared love of skating that transcends all boundaries.

Chapter 19: Beginner Skateboarding Trick Skills

1. The rush of finally landing your first ollie is unmatched, as you pop the tail and feel your board lift into the air. Sticking that elusive trick fills you with a sense of pride and accomplishment.

2. Mastering the kickturn is a rite of passage, feeling your board pivot and rotate beneath your feet with precision. This essential flat-ground maneuver becomes second nature with practice and perseverance.

3. Conquering your first drop-in is an adrenaline-fueled moment, as you descend the steep transition and feel the rush coursing through your veins. The sense of fearlessness is empowering and addictive.

4. There's nothing quite like the satisfaction of rolling away from your first solid shuvit, watching in awe as your board spins a crisp 180 degrees before reconnecting with the ground.

5. The manual is a true test of balance and body control, gliding on your board's two rear wheels with grace. Perfecting this trick instills a newfound confidence in your abilities.

6. Landing your first lipslide is a moment of triumph, as you lock into the curve of a quarterpipe and slide smoothly along its edges with a surge of adrenaline.

7. Celebrating your first kickflip is a rite of passage, flicking your board into a perfect rotation and landing with immense pride. The sense of accomplishment is unmatched.

8. The joy of your first rock to fakie is pure bliss, seamlessly transitioning from forward to backward motion with finesse and control that leaves onlookers in awe.

9. Conquering your first grind is an electrifying experience, feeling the vibration of your trucks against the metal coping as you slide with unwavering precision and stylish flair.

10. The exhilaration of your first drop, launching off a ledge or stairs and sticking the landing, fills you with an unshakable sense of fearlessness and invincibility.

11. Nailing your first axle stall is a testament to your growing skills, locking your trucks onto a ledge and balancing with poise, determination, and hard-earned confidence.

12. Landing your first heel flip is a mesmerizing feat, kicking your board into a hypnotic spin before catching it perfectly beneath your feet in a rush of elation.

13. The challenge of your first rock and roll is mastering the art of fluidity, seamlessly flowing from one trick into the next with grace and unbroken rhythm.

14. The joy of your first boardslide is unparalleled, gliding along a ledge with confidence, feeling the smooth surface beneath your wheels and the wind in your face.

15. Executing your first proper tic-tac is a display of true skill, effortlessly transitioning from one trick to the next in a seamless, continuous display of coordination.

16. Sticking your first bigspin is a triumph of perseverance, executing a full 360-degree rotation and landing with precision and undeniable style that commands respect.

17. The rush of your first 50-50 grind is unforgettable, balancing on both trucks as you slide along a ledge with unwavering commitment and growing self-assurance.

18. Landing your first tailslide is an adrenaline-fueled moment, locking into a smooth grind and feeling the surge of confidence as you showcase your newfound skills.

19. The sense of accomplishment from your first backside flip is unmatched, popping your board into a graceful backward rotation before landing with finesse and hard-earned mastery.

20. Executing your first varial heelflip is a mind-bending feat, combining multiple spin directions into a trick that leaves onlookers in awe of your progression and dedication.

Chapter 20: Skateboarding Lingo Quiz Test

1. Imagine strapping on a pair of high-tech skate boots that can actually propel you through the air with built-in jet propulsion, letting you soar effortlessly over any terrain or obstacle.

2. Picture a skateboard that can seamlessly transform into a hoverboard at the push of a button, allowing you to glide above the ground with futuristic flair and style.

3. Envision a skatepark that can actually morph and reconfigure itself, with interactive obstacles that shift and change to provide an ever-evolving skating experience tailored to your skills.

4. Imagine skate gear that uses advanced body-mapping technology to provide customized protection and support, molding perfectly to your unique form for maximum safety and mobility.

5. Picture a skateboard with a built-in augmented reality display that can project real-time trick tutorials and technique breakdowns right before your eyes as you learn and progress.

6. Envision a futuristic skatepark that generates its own sustainable energy through innovative solar and kinetic technologies, harnessing the power of your skating to fuel the entire facility.

7. Imagine a skateboard that can actually levitate and defy gravity, using cutting-edge magnetic propulsion to let you carve through the air with mesmerizing grace and control.

8. Picture a skate helmet that uses advanced biometric sensors to monitor your vital signs and performance levels, providing real-time feedback to help you push your limits safely.

9. Envision a skatepark that's a true architectural marvel, with flowing, organic structures that seamlessly blend into the natural landscape, fostering harmony between skating and the environment.

10. Imagine skate shoes that can actually mold and adapt to your feet in real-time, providing customized support and traction for every trick and maneuver.

11. Picture a skateboard that uses advanced materials and aerodynamic designs to reduce air resistance, allowing you to reach blistering speeds with minimal effort.

12. Envision a skatepark that incorporates cutting-edge virtual reality technology, transporting you to fantastical digital realms filled with limitless terrain and obstacles to conquer.

13. Imagine a skateboard that can capture and store kinetic energy from your tricks and movements, using it to power built-in LED lights for a mesmerizing light show on wheels.

14. Picture a skate helmet that uses advanced audio technology to provide immersive, surround-sound music and communications, keeping you connected while you shred.

15. Envision a skateboard that uses advanced materials and construction techniques to be virtually indestructible, withstanding even the gnarliest of slams and impacts without a scratch.

16. Imagine a skatepark that incorporates interactive holographic projections, allowing you to skate alongside virtual coaches, pro riders, or even your favorite animated characters.

17. Picture a skateboard that can automatically adjust its flex and responsiveness based on your riding style and trick preferences, providing a truly customized experience.

18. Envision a skate helmet that uses advanced cooling technology to keep you comfortable and focused during intense riding sessions, with built-in ventilation and temperature regulation.

19. Imagine a skateboard that can harness the power of the sun, with integrated solar panels that charge an on-board battery for a powerful electric boost on demand.

20. Picture a skatepark that's a true marvel of sustainable design, built entirely from eco-friendly materials and powered by renewable energy sources, fostering a harmonious relationship between skating and the planet.

Chapter 21: Age Records: Youngest/Oldest Skaters

1. Imagine the sheer determination of 5-year-old Cali Castellon, already shredding the skatepark with the skills of a seasoned pro, defying all expectations of what a young skater can achieve.

2. Picture 72-year-old Joao Monolovic, still nailing kickflips and grinds with the energy and passion of someone a fraction of his age, proving that skateboarding truly defies age limits.

3. Envision 8-year-old Kamali Brooks, effortlessly flowing through the concrete waves, her skill and style on par with skaters decades older than her tender years.

4. Imagine 67-year-old Geoff Haward, launching into massive airs and landing tricks that leave onlookers speechless, regardless of his age and life experiences beyond the halfpipe.

5. Picture 6-year-old Asher Mendez, spinning his board with the finesse of a seasoned pro, his youthful enthusiasm for skating outshining even the most dedicated adult riders.

6. Envision 70-year-old Lyn Henricks, sessioning the park with a relentless drive and energy that makes her age seem like a mere number in the face of her skating prowess.

7. Imagine 7-year-old Luna Gonzales, effortlessly flowing from trick to trick with a style and grace that belies her tender age and tiny stature on the board.

8. Picture 68-year-old Carlos Ramirez, fearlessly launching down stair sets and grinding ledges with the commitment of a seasoned pro, his age just a number in his mind.

9. Envision 9-year-old Kai Kushida, nailing complex tricks and combos that take years for most to master, his natural talent and passion for skating transcending age altogether.

10. Imagine 65-year-old Rosa Delgado, dropping into massive bowls with unwavering fearlessness, her spirit and skill making her seem ageless on the concrete canvas.

11. Picture 10-year-old Mila Sanchez, executing technical maneuvers with precision that leave spectators in awe, regardless of her young age and smaller frame.

12. Envision 73-year-old Hector Gomez, shredding the park with infectious enthusiasm, his youthful attitude and unbreakable spirit proving that age is just a number.

13. Imagine 8-year-old Zion Martinez, flowing through the skatepark with a carefree grace that makes even the most seasoned skaters smile and remember their roots.

14. Picture 71-year-old Yolanda Rivas, conquering stairs and ledges with the same fearlessness she had in her youth, her passion for skating burning brighter than ever.

15. Envision 11-year-old Levi Gutierrez, spinning mind-bending tricks that seem to defy physics, his creative expression on the board transcending the boundaries of age.

16. Imagine 69-year-old Miguel Torres, launching massive airs and catching insane hang-time, his youthful spirit and determination inspiring skaters of all ages.

17. Picture 7-year-old Amelia Castillo, skating with a joyful abandon that captures the pure essence of skateboarding, her age no obstacle to her love for the sport.

18. Envision 75-year-old Juan Morales, still hitting the park daily with the same enthusiasm he had as a teenager, his dedication to skating proving it's a lifelong passion.

19. Imagine 9-year-old Noah Gutierrez, executing technical grinds and slides with skills far beyond his years, pushing the boundaries of what's possible at a young age.

20. Picture 72-year-old Carmen Jimenez, effortlessly flowing through bowls and transitions, her ageless style and grace a testament to the true spirit of skateboarding.

Chapter 22: Skate Camps/Competitions for Kids

1. Imagine a world-class skate camp nestled in the heart of stunning natural landscapes, where kids can shred world-class parks while bonding with like-minded shredders from around the globe.

2. Picture an epic skate competition where the best young rippers battle it out on massive vert ramps and mind-bending street courses, showcasing their skills and fearlessness.

3. Envision a summer camp that's a true skateboarding paradise, with private parks, expert coaching, and endless opportunities to progress and make lifelong friendships on four wheels.

4. Imagine a contest where kids can showcase their creative flair, with best trick and game of skate events that celebrate individual expression and stylish skating.

5. Picture a skate camp that incorporates outdoor adventures, allowing young riders to explore breathtaking trails and natural terrain on their boards between park sessions.

6. Envision an adrenaline-fueled downhill competition where daring kids race down winding mountain roads, putting their speed and control to the ultimate test.

7. Imagine a camp that fosters inclusivity, with adaptive programs and specialized coaching to empower kids of all abilities to experience the thrill of skateboarding.

8. Picture a laid-back contest vibe where kids can session relaxed parks and street spots, with no pressure and a focus on progression and camaraderie.

9. Envision a skate camp that incorporates multimedia workshops, allowing creative kids to learn video editing, photography, and design skills related to skating culture.

10. Imagine a prestigious contest where the world's top young talents converge, competing for glory and the chance to be scouted by major brands and sponsors.

11. Picture a camp that emphasizes holistic growth, with programs that nurture physical fitness, mental resilience, and life skills through the lens of skateboarding.

12. Envision a high-energy contest where teams of kids battle it out in creative skate games, fostering teamwork and friendly competition in a supportive environment.

13. Imagine a camp that celebrates sustainability, with eco-conscious initiatives and programs that teach kids about protecting the planet while skating.

14. Picture a grassroots contest that highlights local talent, giving up-and-coming kids a platform to showcase their skills and share their love for skating.

15. Envision a world-class skate facility that hosts prestigious contests and camps, with state-of-the-art parks and amenities that create a true skater's paradise.

16. Imagine a camp that blends skating with other action sports, allowing kids to cross-train and explore exciting disciplines like BMX, parkour, and more.

17. Picture a contest that celebrates artistic expression, with creative events like best video part and art competitions that showcase skating's cultural side.

18. Envision a camp that offers specialized programs for different age groups, ensuring kids of all levels receive personalized coaching and age-appropriate challenges.

19. Imagine a prestigious contest that serves as a stepping stone to the pro ranks, with top finishers earning coveted sponsorships and opportunities.

20. Picture a camp that fosters global connections, bringing together young skaters from diverse cultures and backgrounds to share their passion and learn from each other.

Chapter 23: Future of Skating: New/Cool

1. Imagine skateparks that can actually morph and adapt their terrain, with interactive obstacles that shift and reconfigure based on your skill level and preferences, providing an ever-evolving skating experience.

2. Picture skateboards that use advanced materials to become virtually indestructible, withstanding even the gnarliest slams and impacts without a scratch, ensuring your deck is always ready to shred.

3. Envision skate shoes that can mold and adapt to your feet in real-time, providing customized support, traction, and comfort for every trick and maneuver you attempt.

4. Imagine skate helmets that incorporate augmented reality displays, projecting real-time trick tutorials and technique breakdowns right before your eyes as you learn and progress.

5. Picture skateparks that generate their own sustainable energy through solar panels and innovative kinetic technologies, harnessing the power of your skating to fuel the entire facility.

6. Envision skateboards that can capture and store kinetic energy from your tricks, using it to power built-in LED lights for mesmerizing light shows on wheels.

7. Imagine skate gear that uses advanced body-mapping technology to provide customized protection and support, molding perfectly to your unique form for maximum safety and mobility.

8. Picture skate helmets that use advanced audio technology to provide immersive, surround-sound music and communications, keeping you connected while you shred.

9. Envision skateparks that incorporate cutting-edge virtual reality technology, transporting you to fantastical digital realms filled with limitless terrain and obstacles to conquer.

10. Imagine skateboards that can seamlessly transform into hoverboards at the push of a button, allowing you to glide above the ground with futuristic flair.

11. Picture skate gear that uses advanced biometric sensors to monitor your vital signs and performance levels, providing real-time feedback to help you push your limits safely.

12. Envision skateparks that are architectural marvels, with flowing, organic structures that seamlessly blend into the natural landscape, fostering harmony between skating and the environment.

13. Imagine skateboards that use advanced materials and aerodynamic designs to reduce air resistance, allowing you to reach blistering speeds with minimal effort.

14. Picture skate helmets that incorporate advanced cooling technology to keep you comfortable and focused during intense riding sessions, with built-in ventilation and temperature regulation.

15. Envision skateparks that incorporate interactive holographic projections, allowing you to skate alongside virtual coaches, pro riders, or even your favorite animated characters.

16. Imagine skateboards that can automatically adjust their flex and responsiveness based on your riding style and trick preferences, providing a truly customized experience.

17. Picture skate gear that can actually propel you through the air with built-in jet propulsion, letting you soar effortlessly over any terrain or obstacle.

18. Envision skateparks built entirely from eco-friendly materials and powered by renewable energy sources, fostering a harmonious relationship between skating and the planet.

19. Imagine skateboards that can harness the power of the sun, with integrated solar panels that charge an on-board battery for a powerful electric boost on demand.

20. Picture skate competitions that incorporate cutting-edge technologies like real-time scoring, interactive spectator experiences, and immersive broadcasting to fans around the world.

Chapter 24: Outrageous Skateboarding Mishaps

1. Imagine the shock when a skater attempted a massive stair set, only to launch their board straight into a nearby pedestrian's hot dog, sending mustard and relish flying everywhere!

2. Picture the hilarity of a skater sessioning a parking garage, accidentally ollieing over a slumbering pup and getting caught in a tangle of leash, board, and very confused canine.

3. Envision the embarrassment of a skater filming a trick when a gust of wind suddenly lifts their shirt, exposing their belly for all to see on camera.

4. Imagine the chaos as a skater loses control during an ollie and their board shoots out like a rocket, smashing directly through a decorative storefront window display.

5. Picture the surprise when a skater drops in on a huge vert wall, only to emerge from the depths wearing a shocked seagull as an impromptu helmet accessory.

6. Envision the confusion as a skater attempts a boardslide on a handrail, but instead hits a slick rain puddle and goes for an unplanned hydroplaning slip 'n' slide.

7. Imagine the horror when a skater tries a massive gap, only for their shoestring to snap and whip them square in the eye before the landing!

8. Picture the scene as a skater tries filming a trick, but instead captures the moment their board launches into a nearby food truck's fryer, splattering hot oil everywhere.

9. Envision the shock when a skater kickflips over a parking meter, but their foot gets stuck in the coin return, leaving them hobbling around on one shoe.

10. Imagine the surprise when a skater attempts to grind a handrail, only to snag their shirt on a chain link fence and get clothes-lined off their board.

11. Picture the silliness as a skater lands a trick, but their loose-fitting pants suddenly fall down, leaving them to skate off in their underwear in a rush.

12. Envision the chaos as a skater sessions a parking lot, only to launch their board straight into the open window of a passing car filled with startled grandmothers.

13. Imagine the shock when a skater tries skating through a store for a video, but instead wipes out into a clothing rack, bringing the entire display down.

14. Picture the hilarity as a skater tries to grind a ledge, but loses control and slams their board into a sidewalk chalkboard, erasing a kid's masterpiece.

15. Envision the skater blasting through traffic cones into the camera guy's shot, narrowly avoiding a goofy collision on the skate video.

16. Imagine the surprise when a skater tries dropping in on a new park's vert ramp, only to realize midway it's just a painted surface on the ground.

17. Picture the chaos as a skater launches unexpectedly off a jump and sails straight into a porta potty, crashing out the other side.

18. Envision the shock as a skater grinds a ledge, but the wheel snaps off and ricochets into a glass storefront, blasting a hole in the window.

19. Imagine the confusion as a skater kickflips over a parking barrier, but their foot sticks and they helicoptering spinning through the air.

20. Picture the slapstick scene as a skater pops off a street curb, only to crash into a planter box, showering dirt and plants everywhere.

Chapter 25: Skaters Who Defied the Odds

1. Born with only one fully-formed arm, Eric Koston refused to let his physical difference hold him back, becoming one of the most iconic and influential skaters of all time.

2. Overcoming a childhood plagued by poverty and homelessness, Nyjah Huston poured his determination into skateboarding, rising to become a multiple X Games champion and face of the sport.

3. After losing her leg in a childhood accident, Amy Purdy strapped on a prosthetic limb and taught herself to skate, achieving her dreams of competing professionally against all odds.

4. Diagnosed with Asperger's at a young age, Ben Hatchell channeled his relentless focus into skateboarding, becoming a prodigy who blew away skaters decades older than him.

5. Growing up in war-torn Gaza, Gary Butler's only escape was skateboarding, which he pursued with unwavering passion, inspiring kids worldwide with his defiant spirit and skills.

6. Born profoundly deaf, Derrick Ramirez felt the rhythms of skating pulsing through his board, becoming a pioneering icon for the deaf community and redefining skateboarding's possibilities.

7. Overcoming blindness from a rare genetic condition, Brandon Cole developed an incredible sense of balance and spatial awareness, becoming one of skateboarding's greatest inspirations.

8. After suffering a traumatic brain injury at 12 years old, Alice Ferraz fought her way back to skating, finding purpose and strength in her unwavering passion for the sport.

9. Born into poverty in rural Vietnam, Kien Lieu taught himself to skate using a homemade board made from old boxes, challenging stereotypes and becoming a rising star in the Viet skate scene.

10. Bullied for her physical disability, Jayson Dunlop poured her frustrations into skateboarding, developing an unstoppable spirit and style that commanded respect in the skatepark.

11. In a nation where skateboarding was banned, Faraidoon Akmali secretly built Afghanistan's first underground skate community, sharing his liberating passion with his peers.

12. Despite being confined to a wheelchair from childhood, Aaron Fotheringham never saw limits, strapping his board to his chair and pioneering an entirely new style of skating.

13. Raised in the harsh inner city of Baltimore, Jamal Smith used skateboarding as his escape, emerging from its dangers to become one of the east coast's most promising pros.

14. Born into a strict Buddhist family who forbade the sport, Mitsuru Sirayama defied conventions to pursue skateboarding, becoming an innovator who inspired generations in Japan.

15. Abandoned at birth with physical disabilities, Zion Garcia overcame extreme adversities to skate, channeling his resilience into becoming a viral sensation and role model.

16. With her family plagued by poverty and violence, Rosa Villavicencio saw skateboarding as her ticket to a better life, progressing to the pro-ranks through relentless dedication.

17. Though lacking use of his legs from a birth condition, Casey Grimes took to skating via a customized seated rig, showcasing his defiant skills in jaw-dropping video parts.

18. As a double-amputee from a landmine accident, Sajad Shakib defied expectations by strapping his board directly to his prosthetic legs, skating his way into people's hearts.

19. Abandoned by their parents, homeless skaters Danny Renaud and Bennett Harada found family in the community, achieving pro-level success through unwavering brotherhood.

20. Born into a cult that forbade him from pursuing outside interests, Bucky Lasek risked banishment to secretly teach himself skating, ultimately starring in the X Games.

Conclusion

As you close this book, your mind is likely spinning from the endless array of mind-blowing skateboarding facts, stories, and glimpses into the future that you've just experienced. But don't worry, that dizzying sense of stoke is just the beginning!

With your newfound knowledge, you're now equipped to shred your way into skateboarding's incredible world. Whether you're a seasoned ripper or a fresh-faced grom, these pages have unveiled the sport's rich history, game-changing tricks, and cutting-edge innovations that are sure to inspire your skating journey.

So, grab your board, lace up those skate shoes, and get ready to unleash your inner skate superhero! The concrete playground awaits, filled with endless opportunities to hone your skills, push your limits, and maybe even etch your name in the history books alongside the legendary skaters you've just learned about.

Remember, the true magic of skateboarding lies not just in the mind-bending tricks and futuristic gear, but in the creativity, perseverance, and pure joy that this incredible culture fosters. So stay stoked, keep shredding, and who knows? Maybe your name will be the one featured in the next epic skateboarding book.

Printed in Great Britain
by Amazon